بِسْمِ اللَّهِ الرَّحْمٰنِ الرَّحِيمِ

Bismi Allahi Ar-Rahmani Ar-Rahimee

In the name of Allah, the Most Merciful, the Most Merciful

Surah Yaseen

Surah Yasin in Arabic, English and Transliteration
with Benefits

Surah Al Fatiha (the Opener) الفاتحة

Bismi Allāhi Ar-Raĥmāni Ar-Raĥīmi
(1) «In the name of God, the Gracious, the Merciful.»

١ـ بِسْمِ اللَّهِ الرَّحْمٰنِ الرَّحِيمِ

Al-Ĥamdu Lillāhi Rabbi Al-`Ālamīna
(2) « Praise be to God, Lord of the Worlds.»

٢ـ الْحَمْدُ لِلَّهِ رَبِّ الْعَالَمِينَ

Ar-Raĥmāni Ar-Raĥīmi
(3) «The Most Gracious, the Most Merciful.»

٣ـ الرَّحْمٰنِ الرَّحِيمِ

Māliki Yawmi Ad-Dīni
(4) Master of the Day of Judgment.»

٤ـ مَالِكِ يَوْمِ الدِّينِ

'Īyāka Na`budu Wa 'Īyāka Nasta`īnu
(5) «It is You we worship, and upon You we call for help.»

٥ـ إِيَّاكَ نَعْبُدُ وَإِيَّاكَ نَسْتَعِينُ

Ihdinā Aş-Şirāţa Al-Mustaqīma
(6) «Guide us to the straight path.»

٦ـ اهْدِنَا الصِّرَاطَ الْمُسْتَقِيمَ

Şirāţa Al-Ladhīna 'An`amta `Alayhim Ghayri Al-Maghđūbi `Alayhim Wa Lā Ađ-Đāllīna
(6) «The path of those You have blessed, not of those against whom there is anger, nor of those who are misguided.»

٧ صِرَاطَ الَّذِينَ أَنْعَمْتَ عَلَيْهِمْ غَيْرِ الْمَغْضُوبِ عَلَيْهِمْ وَلَا الضَّالِّينَ

Surah Yaseen: Arabic & Phonetic

Bismi Allāhi Ar-Raĥmāni Ar-Raĥīmi	بِسْمِ اللهِ الرَّحْمٰنِ الرَّحِيمِ
(1) Yā -Sīn	١ـ يس
(2) Wa Al-Qur'āni Al-Ĥakīmi	٢ـ وَالْقُرْآنِ الْحَكِيمِ
(3) 'Innaka Lamina Al-Mursalīna	٣ـ إِنَّكَ لَمِنَ الْمُرْسَلِينَ
(4) `Alá Şirāţin Mustaqīmin	٤ـ عَلَى صِرَاطٍ مُسْتَقِيمٍ
(5) Tanzīla Al-`Azīzi Ar-Raĥīmi	٥ـ تَنْزِيلَ الْعَزِيزِ الرَّحِيمِ
(6) Litundhira Qawmāan Mā 'Undhira 'Ābā'uuhum Fahum Ghāfilūna	٦ـ لِتُنْذِرَ قَوْمًا مَا أُنْذِرَ آبَاؤُهُمْ فَهُمْ غَافِلُونَ
(7) Laqad Ĥaqqa Al-Qawlu `Alá 'Aktharihim Fahum Lā Yu'uminūna	٧ـ لَقَدْ حَقَّ الْقَوْلُ عَلَى أَكْثَرِهِمْ فَهُمْ لَا يُؤْمِنُونَ
(8) 'Innā Ja`alnā Fī 'A`nāqihim 'Aghlālāan Fahiya 'Ilá Al-'Adhqāni Fahum Muqmaĥūna	٨ـ إِنَّا جَعَلْنَا فِي أَعْنَاقِهِمْ أَغْلَالًا فَهِيَ إِلَى الْأَذْقَانِ فَهُمْ مُقْمَحُونَ
(9) Wa Ja`alnā Min Bayni 'Aydīhim Saddāan Wa Min Khalfihim Saddāan	٩ـ وَجَعَلْنَا مِنْ بَيْنِ أَيْدِيهِمْ سَدًّا وَمِنْ خَلْفِهِمْ سَدًّا فَأَغْشَيْنَاهُمْ فَهُمْ لَا يُبْصِرُونَ

Fa'aghshaynāhum Fahum Lā
Yubşirūna

(10) Wa Sawā'un `Alayhim
'A'andhartahum 'Am Lam
Tundhirhum Lā Yu'uminūna

١٠ـ وَسَوَاءٌ عَلَيْهِمْ أَأَنْذَرْتَهُمْ أَمْ لَمْ تُنْذِرْهُمْ لَا
يُؤْمِنُونَ

(11) 'Innamā Tundhiru Mani
Attaba`a Adh-Dhikra Wa Khashiya
Ar-Raĥmana Bil-Ghaybi
Fabashirhu Bimaghfiratin Wa
'Ajrin Karīmin

١١ـ إِنَّمَا تُنْذِرُ مَنِ اتَّبَعَ الذِّكْرَ وَخَشِيَ
الرَّحْمَٰنَ بِالْغَيْبِ ۖ فَبَشِّرْهُ بِمَغْفِرَةٍ وَأَجْرٍ كَرِيمٍ

(12) 'Innā Naĥnu Nuĥyi Al-Mawtá
Wa Naktubu Mā Qaddamū Wa
'Āthārahum Wa Kulla Shay'in
'Ĥşaynāhu Fī 'Imāmin Mubīnin

١٢ـ إِنَّا نَحْنُ نُحْيِي الْمَوْتَىٰ وَنَكْتُبُ مَا قَدَّمُوا
وَآثَارَهُمْ ۚ وَكُلَّ شَيْءٍ أَحْصَيْنَاهُ فِي إِمَامٍ مُبِينٍ

(13) Wa Ađrib Lahum Mathalāan
'Aşĥāba Al-Qaryati 'Idh Jā'ahā Al-
Mursalūna

١٣ـ وَاضْرِبْ لَهُمْ مَثَلًا أَصْحَابَ الْقَرْيَةِ إِذْ
جَاءَهَا الْمُرْسَلُونَ

(14) 'Idh 'Arsalnā 'Ilayhimu
Athnayni Fakadhabūhumā
Fa`azzaznā Bithālithin Faqālū 'Innā
'Ilaykum Mursalūna

١٤ـ إِذْ أَرْسَلْنَا إِلَيْهِمُ اثْنَيْنِ فَكَذَّبُوهُمَا فَعَزَّزْنَا
بِثَالِثٍ فَقَالُوا إِنَّا إِلَيْكُمْ مُرْسَلُونَ

(15) Qālū Mā 'Antum 'Illā Basharun Mithlunā Wa Mā 'Anzala Ar-Raĥmānu Min Shay'in 'In 'Antum 'Illā Takdhibūna	١٥ـ قَالُوا مَا أَنْتُمْ إِلَّا بَشَرٌ مِثْلُنَا وَمَا أَنْزَلَ الرَّحْمَٰنُ مِنْ شَيْءٍ إِنْ أَنْتُمْ إِلَّا تَكْذِبُونَ
(16) Qālū Rabbunā Ya`lamu 'Innā 'Ilaykum Lamursalūna	١٦ـ قَالُوا رَبُّنَا يَعْلَمُ إِنَّا إِلَيْكُمْ لَمُرْسَلُونَ
(17) Wa Mā `Alaynā 'Illā Al-Balāghu Al-Mubīnu	١٧ـ وَمَا عَلَيْنَا إِلَّا الْبَلَاغُ الْمُبِينُ
(18) Qālū 'Innā Taţayyarnā Bikum La'in Lam Tantahū Lanarjuman-nakum Wa Layamassannakum Minnā `Adhābun 'Alīmun	١٨ـ قَالُوا إِنَّا تَطَيَّرْنَا بِكُمْ لَئِنْ لَمْ تَنْتَهُوا لَنَرْجُمَنَّكُمْ وَلَيَمَسَّنَّكُمْ مِنَّا عَذَابٌ أَلِيمٌ
(19) Qālū Ţā'irukum Ma`akum 'A'in Dhukkirtum Bal 'Antum Qawmun Musrifūna	١٩ـ قَالُوا طَائِرُكُمْ مَعَكُمْ أَئِنْ ذُكِّرْتُمْ بَلْ أَنْتُمْ قَوْمٌ مُسْرِفُونَ
(20) Wa Jā'a Min 'Aqşá Al-Madīnati Rajulun Yas`á Qāla Yā Qawmi Attabi`ū Al-Mursalīna	٢٠ـ وَجَاءَ مِنْ أَقْصَى الْمَدِينَةِ رَجُلٌ يَسْعَىٰ قَالَ يَا قَوْمِ اتَّبِعُوا الْمُرْسَلِينَ
(21) Attabi`ū Man Lā Yas'alukum 'Ajrāan Wa Hum Muhtadūna	٢١ـ اتَّبِعُوا مَنْ لَا يَسْأَلُكُمْ أَجْرًا وَهُمْ مُهْتَدُونَ

(22) Wa Mā Liya Lā 'A`budu Al-Ladhī Faṭaranī Wa 'Ilayhi Turja`ūna	٢٢ـ وَمَا لِيَ لَا أَعْبُدُ الَّذِي فَطَرَنِي وَإِلَيْهِ تُرْجَعُونَ
(23) 'A'attakhidhu Min Dūnihi 'Ālihatan 'In Yuridni Ar-Raĥmānu Biđurrin Lā Tughni `Annī Shafā`atuhum Shay'āan Wa Lā Yunqidhūni	٢٣ـ أَأَتَّخِذُ مِنْ دُونِهِ آلِهَةً إِنْ يُرِدْنِ الرَّحْمَنُ بِضُرٍّ لَا تُغْنِ عَنِّي شَفَاعَتُهُمْ شَيْئًا وَلَا يُنْقِذُونِ
(24) 'Innī 'Idhāan Lafī Đalālin Mubīnin	٢٤ـ إِنِّي إِذًا لَفِي ضَلَالٍ مُبِينٍ
(25) 'Innī 'Āmantu Birabbikum Fāsma`ūni	٢٥ـ إِنِّي آمَنْتُ بِرَبِّكُمْ فَاسْمَعُونِ
(26) Qīla Adkhuli Al-Jannata Qāla Yā Layta Qawmī Ya`lamūna	٢٦ـ قِيلَ ادْخُلِ الْجَنَّةَ ۖ قَالَ يَا لَيْتَ قَوْمِي يَعْلَمُونَ
(27) Bimā Ghafara Lī Rabbī Wa Ja`alanī Mina Al-Mukramīna	٢٧ـ بِمَا غَفَرَ لِي رَبِّي وَجَعَلَنِي مِنَ الْمُكْرَمِينَ
(28) Wa Mā 'Anzalnā `Alá Qawmihi Min Ba`dihi Min Jundin Mina As-Samā'i Wa Mā Kunnā Munzilīna	٢٨ـ وَمَا أَنْزَلْنَا عَلَىٰ قَوْمِهِ مِنْ بَعْدِهِ مِنْ جُنْدٍ مِنَ السَّمَاءِ وَمَا كُنَّا مُنْزِلِينَ

(29) 'In Kānat 'Illā Şayĥatan Wāĥidatan Fa'idhā Hum Khāmidūna	٢٩- إِنْ كَانَتْ إِلَّا صَيْحَةً وَاحِدَةً فَإِذَا هُمْ خَامِدُونَ
(30) Yā Ĥasratan `Alá Al-`Ibādi Mā Ya'tīhim Min Rasūlin 'Illā Kānū Bihi Yastahzi'ūn	٣٠- يَا حَسْرَةً عَلَى الْعِبَادِ ۚ مَا يَأْتِيهِمْ مِنْ رَسُولٍ إِلَّا كَانُوا بِهِ يَسْتَهْزِئُونَ
(31) 'Alam Yaraw Kam 'Ahlaknā Qablahum Mina Al-Qurūni 'Annahum 'Ilayhim Lā Yarji`ūna	٣١- أَلَمْ يَرَوْا كَمْ أَهْلَكْنَا قَبْلَهُمْ مِنَ الْقُرُونِ أَنَّهُمْ إِلَيْهِمْ لَا يَرْجِعُونَ
(32) Wa 'In Kullun Lammā Jamī`un Ladaynā Muĥđarūna	٣٢- وَإِنْ كُلٌّ لَمَّا جَمِيعٌ لَدَيْنَا مُحْضَرُونَ
(33) Wa 'Āyatun Lahumu Al-'Arđu Al-Maytatu 'Aĥyaynāhā Wa 'Akhrajnā Minhā Ĥabbāan Faminhu Ya'kulūna	٣٣- وَآيَةٌ لَهُمُ الْأَرْضُ الْمَيْتَةُ أَحْيَيْنَاهَا وَأَخْرَجْنَا مِنْهَا حَبًّا فَمِنْهُ يَأْكُلُونَ
(34) Wa Ja`alnā Fīhā Jannātin Min Nakhīlin Wa 'A`nābin Wa Fajjarnā Fīhā Mina Al-`Uyūni	٣٤- وَجَعَلْنَا فِيهَا جَنَّاتٍ مِنْ نَخِيلٍ وَأَعْنَابٍ وَفَجَّرْنَا فِيهَا مِنَ الْعُيُونِ
(35) Liya'kulū Min Thamarihi Wa Mā `Amilat/hu 'Aydīhim 'Afalā Yashkurūna	٣٥- لِيَأْكُلُوا مِنْ ثَمَرِهِ وَمَا عَمِلَتْهُ أَيْدِيهِمْ ۖ أَفَلَا يَشْكُرُونَ

(36) Subĥāna Al-Ladhī Khalaqa Al-'Azwāja Kullahā Mimmā Tunbitu Al-'Arđu Wa Min 'Anfusihim Wa Mimmā Lā Ya`lamūna	٣٦ـ سُبْحَانَ الَّذِي خَلَقَ الْأَزْوَاجَ كُلَّهَا مِمَّا تُنْبِتُ الْأَرْضُ وَمِنْ أَنْفُسِهِمْ وَمِمَّا لَا يَعْلَمُونَ
(37) Wa 'Āyatun Lahumu Al-Laylu Naslakhu Minhu An-Nahāra Fa'idhā Hum Mužlimūna	٣٧ـ وَآيَةٌ لَهُمُ اللَّيْلُ نَسْلَخُ مِنْهُ النَّهَارَ فَإِذَا هُمْ مُظْلِمُونَ
(38) Wa Ash-Shamsu Tajrī Limustaqarrin Lahā Dhālika Taqdīru Al-`Azīzi Al-`Alīmi	٣٨ـ وَالشَّمْسُ تَجْرِي لِمُسْتَقَرٍّ لَهَا ۚ ذَٰلِكَ تَقْدِيرُ الْعَزِيزِ الْعَلِيمِ
(39) Wa Al-Qamara Qaddarnāhu Manāzila Ĥattá `Āda Kāl`urjūni Al-Qadīmi	٣٩ـ وَالْقَمَرَ قَدَّرْنَاهُ مَنَازِلَ حَتَّىٰ عَادَ كَالْعُرْجُونِ الْقَدِيمِ
(40) Lā Ash-Shamsu Yanbaghī Lahā 'An Tudrika Al-Qamara Wa Lā Al-Laylu Sābiqu An-Nahāri Wa Kullun Fī Falakin Yasbaĥūna	٤٠ـ لَا الشَّمْسُ يَنْبَغِي لَهَا أَنْ تُدْرِكَ الْقَمَرَ وَلَا اللَّيْلُ سَابِقُ النَّهَارِ ۚ وَكُلٌّ فِي فَلَكٍ يَسْبَحُونَ
(41) Wa 'Āyatun Lahum 'Annā Ĥamalnā Dhurrīyatahum Fī Al-Fulki Al-Mashĥūni	٤١ـ وَآيَةٌ لَهُمْ أَنَّا حَمَلْنَا ذُرِّيَّتَهُمْ فِي الْفُلْكِ الْمَشْحُونِ
(42) Wa Khalaqnā Lahum Min Mithlihi Mā Yarkabūna	٤٢ـ وَخَلَقْنَا لَهُمْ مِنْ مِثْلِهِ مَا يَرْكَبُونَ

(43) Wa 'In Nasha' Nughriqhum Falā Şarīkha Lahum Wa Lā Hum Yunqadhūna	٤٣ـ وَإِنْ نَشَأْ نُغْرِقْهُمْ فَلَا صَرِيخَ لَهُمْ وَلَا هُمْ يُنْقَذُونَ
(44) 'Illā Raĥmatan Minnā Wa Matā`āan 'Ilá Ĥīnin	٤٤ـ إِلَّا رَحْمَةً مِنَّا وَمَتَاعًا إِلَى حِينٍ
(45) Wa 'Idhā Qīla Lahumu Atta-qū Mā Bayna 'Aydīkum Wa Mā Khalfakum La`allakum Turĥamūna	٤٥ـ وَإِذَا قِيلَ لَهُمُ اتَّقُوا مَا بَيْنَ أَيْدِيكُمْ وَمَا خَلْفَكُمْ لَعَلَّكُمْ تُرْحَمُونَ
(46) Wa Mā Ta'tīhim Min 'Āyatin Min 'Āyāti Rabbihim 'Illā Kānū `Anhā Mu`riđīna	٤٦ـ وَمَا تَأْتِيهِمْ مِنْ آيَةٍ مِنْ آيَاتِ رَبِّهِمْ إِلَّا كَانُوا عَنْهَا مُعْرِضِينَ
(47) Wa 'Idhā Qīla Lahum 'Anfiqū Mimmā Razaqakumu Allāhu Qāla Al-Ladhīna Kafarū Lilladhīna 'Āmanū 'Anuṭ`imu Man Law Yashā'u Allāhu 'Aṭ`amahu 'In 'Antum 'Illā Fī Đalālin Mubīnin	٤٧ـ وَإِذَا قِيلَ لَهُمْ أَنْفِقُوا مِمَّا رَزَقَكُمُ اللَّهُ قَالَ الَّذِينَ كَفَرُوا لِلَّذِينَ آمَنُوا أَنُطْعِمُ مَنْ لَوْ يَشَاءُ اللَّهُ أَطْعَمَهُ إِنْ أَنْتُمْ إِلَّا فِي ضَلَالٍ مُبِينٍ
(48) Wa Yaqūlūna Matá Hādhā Al-Wa`du 'In Kuntum Şādiqīna	٤٨ـ وَيَقُولُونَ مَتَى هَذَا الْوَعْدُ إِنْ كُنْتُمْ صَادِقِينَ
(49) Mā Yanzurūna 'Illā Şayĥatan Wāĥidatan Ta'khudhuhum Wa Hum Yakhişşimūna	٤٩ـ مَا يَنْظُرُونَ إِلَّا صَيْحَةً وَاحِدَةً تَأْخُذُهُمْ وَهُمْ يَخِصِّمُونَ

(50) Falā Yastaţī`ūna Tawşiyatan Wa Lā 'Ilá 'Ahlihim Yarji`ūna

٥٠ـ فَلَا يَسْتَطِيعُونَ تَوْصِيَةً وَلَا إِلَى أَهْلِهِمْ يَرْجِعُونَ

(51) Wa Nufikha Fī Aş-Şūri Fa'idhā Hum Mina Al-'Ajdāthi 'Ilá Rabbihim Yansilūna

٥١ـ وَنُفِخَ فِي الصُّورِ فَإِذَا هُم مِنَ الْأَجْدَاثِ إِلَى رَبِّهِمْ يَنسِلُونَ

(52) Qālū Yā Waylanā Man Ba`athanā Min Marqadinā Hādhā Mā Wa`ada Ar-Raĥmānu Wa Şadaqa Al-Mursalūna

٥٢ـ قَالُوا يَا وَيْلَنَا مَن بَعَثَنَا مِن مَّرْقَدِنَا ۜ هَٰذَا مَا وَعَدَ الرَّحْمَٰنُ وَصَدَقَ الْمُرْسَلُونَ

(53) 'In Kānat 'Illā Şayĥatan Wāĥidatan Fa'idhā Hum Jamī`un Ladaynā Muĥđarūna

٥٣ـ إِن كَانَتْ إِلَّا صَيْحَةً وَاحِدَةً فَإِذَا هُمْ جَمِيعٌ لَّدَيْنَا مُحْضَرُونَ

(54) Fālyawma Lā Tužlamu Nafsun Shay'āan Wa Lā Tujzawna 'Illā Mā Kuntum Ta`malūna

٥٤ـ فَالْيَوْمَ لَا تُظْلَمُ نَفْسٌ شَيْئًا وَلَا تُجْزَوْنَ إِلَّا مَا كُنتُمْ تَعْمَلُونَ

(55) 'Inna 'Aşĥāba Al-Jannati Al-Yawma Fī Shughulin Fākihūna

٥٥ـ إِنَّ أَصْحَابَ الْجَنَّةِ الْيَوْمَ فِي شُغُلٍ فَاكِهُونَ

(56) Hum Wa 'Azwājuhum Fī Žilālin `Alá Al-'Arā'iki Muttaki'ūna

٥٦ـ هُمْ وَأَزْوَاجُهُمْ فِي ظِلَالٍ عَلَى الْأَرَائِكِ مُتَّكِئُونَ

(57) Lahum Fīhā Fākihatun Wa Lahum Mā Yadda`ūna	٥٧ـ لَهُمْ فِيهَا فَاكِهَةٌ وَلَهُمْ مَا يَدَّعُونَ
(58) Salāmun Qawlāan Min Rabbin Raĥīmin	٥٨ـ سَلَامٌ قَوْلًا مِنْ رَبٍّ رَحِيمٍ
(59) Wa Amtāzū Al-Yawma 'Ayyuhā Al-Mujrimūna	٥٩ـ وَامْتَازُوا الْيَوْمَ أَيُّهَا الْمُجْرِمُونَ
(60) 'Alam 'A`had 'Ilaykum Yā Banī 'Ādama 'An Lā Ta`budū Ash-Shayţāna 'Innahu Lakum `Adūwun Mubīnun	٦٠ـ أَلَمْ أَعْهَدْ إِلَيْكُمْ يَا بَنِي آدَمَ أَنْ لَا تَعْبُدُوا الشَّيْطَانَ ۖ إِنَّهُ لَكُمْ عَدُوٌّ مُبِينٌ
(61) Wa 'Ani A`budūnī Hādhā Şirāţun Mustaqīmun	٦١ـ وَأَنِ اعْبُدُونِي ۚ هَٰذَا صِرَاطٌ مُسْتَقِيمٌ
(62) Wa Laqad 'Ađalla Minkum Jibillāan Kathīrāan 'Afalam Takūnū Ta`qilūna	٦٢ـ وَلَقَدْ أَضَلَّ مِنْكُمْ جِبِلًّا كَثِيرًا ۖ أَفَلَمْ تَكُونُوا تَعْقِلُونَ
(63) Hadhihi Jahannamu Allatī Kuntum Tū`adūna	٦٣ـ هَٰذِهِ جَهَنَّمُ الَّتِي كُنْتُمْ تُوعَدُونَ
(64) Aşlawhā Al-Yawma Bimā Kuntum Takfurūna	٦٤ـ اصْلَوْهَا الْيَوْمَ بِمَا كُنْتُمْ تَكْفُرُونَ

(65) Al-Yawma Nakhtimu `Alá 'Afwāhihim Wa Tukallimunā 'Aydīhim Wa Tash/hadu 'Arjuluhum Bimā Kānū Yaksibūna

٦٥ـ الْيَوْمَ نَخْتِمُ عَلَىٰ أَفْوَاهِهِمْ وَتُكَلِّمُنَا أَيْدِيهِمْ وَتَشْهَدُ أَرْجُلُهُمْ بِمَا كَانُوا يَكْسِبُونَ

(66) Wa Law Nashā'u Laţamasnā `Alá 'A`yunihim Fāstabaqū Aş-Şirāţa Fa'anná Yubşirūna

٦٦ـ وَلَوْ نَشَاءُ لَطَمَسْنَا عَلَىٰ أَعْيُنِهِمْ فَاسْتَبَقُوا الصِّرَاطَ فَأَنَّىٰ يُبْصِرُونَ

(67) Wa Law Nashā'u Lamasakhnāhum `Alá Makānatihim Famā Astaţā`ū Muđīyāan Wa Lā Yarji`ūna

٦٧ـ وَلَوْ نَشَاءُ لَمَسَخْنَاهُمْ عَلَىٰ مَكَانَتِهِمْ فَمَا اسْتَطَاعُوا مُضِيًّا وَلَا يَرْجِعُونَ

(68) Wa Man Nu`ammirhu Nunakkis/hu Fī Al-Khalqi 'Afalā Ya`qilūna

٦٨ـ وَمَنْ نُعَمِّرْهُ نُنَكِّسْهُ فِي الْخَلْقِ ۚ أَفَلَا يَعْقِلُونَ

(69) Wa Mā `Allamnāhu Ash-Shi`ra Wa Mā Yanbaghī Lahu 'In Huwa 'Illā Dhikrun Wa Qur'ānun Mubīnun

٦٩ـ وَمَا عَلَّمْنَاهُ الشِّعْرَ وَمَا يَنْبَغِي لَهُ ۚ إِنْ هُوَ إِلَّا ذِكْرٌ وَقُرْآنٌ مُبِينٌ

(70) Liyundhira Man Kāna Ĥayyāan Wa Yaĥiqqa Al-Qawlu `Alá Al-Kāfirīna

٧٠ـ لِيُنْذِرَ مَنْ كَانَ حَيًّا وَيَحِقَّ الْقَوْلُ عَلَى الْكَافِرِينَ

(71) 'Awalam Yaraw 'Annā Khalaqnā Lahum Mimmā `Amilat 'Aydīnā 'An`āmāan Fahum Lahā Mālikūna	٧١ـ أَوَلَمْ يَرَوْا أَنَّا خَلَقْنَا لَهُمْ مِمَّا عَمِلَتْ أَيْدِينَا أَنْعَامًا فَهُمْ لَهَا مَالِكُونَ
(72) Wa Dhallalnāhā Lahum Faminhā Rakūbuhum Wa Minhā Ya'kulūna	٧٢ـ وَذَلَّلْنَاهَا لَهُمْ فَمِنْهَا رَكُوبُهُمْ وَمِنْهَا يَأْكُلُونَ
(73) Wa Lahum Fīhā Manāfi`u Wa Mashāribu 'Afalā Yashkurūna	٧٣ـ وَلَهُمْ فِيهَا مَنَافِعُ وَمَشَارِبُ ۖ أَفَلَا يَشْكُرُونَ
(74) Wa Attakhadhū Min Dūni Allāhi 'Ālihatan La`allahum Yunşarūna	٧٤ـ وَاتَّخَذُوا مِنْ دُونِ اللَّهِ آلِهَةً لَعَلَّهُمْ يُنْصَرُونَ
(75) Lā Yastaţī`ūna Naşrahum Wa Hum Lahum Jundun Muĥđarūna	٧٥ـ لَا يَسْتَطِيعُونَ نَصْرَهُمْ وَهُمْ لَهُمْ جُنْدٌ مُحْضَرُونَ
(76) Falā Yaĥzunka Qawluhum 'Innā Na`lamu Mā Yusirrūna Wa Mā Yu`linūna	٧٦ـ فَلَا يَحْزُنْكَ قَوْلُهُمْ ۖ إِنَّا نَعْلَمُ مَا يُسِرُّونَ وَمَا يُعْلِنُونَ
(77) 'Awalam Yara Al-'Insānu 'Annā Khalaqnāhu Min Nuţfatin Fa'idhā Huwa Khaşīmun Mubīnun	٧٧ـ أَوَلَمْ يَرَ الْإِنْسَانُ أَنَّا خَلَقْنَاهُ مِنْ نُطْفَةٍ فَإِذَا هُوَ خَصِيمٌ مُبِينٌ

(78) Wa Ḍaraba Lanā Mathalāan Wa Nasiya Khalqahu Qāla Man Yuĥyī Al-`Ižāma Wa Hiya Ramīmun

٧٨ ـ وَضَرَبَ لَنَا مَثَلًا وَنَسِيَ خَلْقَهُ ۖ قَالَ مَنْ يُحْيِي الْعِظَامَ وَهِيَ رَمِيمٌ

(79) Qul Yuĥyīhā Al-Ladhī 'Ansha'ahā 'Awwala Marratin Wa Huwa Bikulli Khalqin `Alīmun

٧٩ ـ قُلْ يُحْيِيهَا الَّذِي أَنْشَأَهَا أَوَّلَ مَرَّةٍ ۖ وَهُوَ بِكُلِّ خَلْقٍ عَلِيمٌ

(80) Al-Ladhī Ja`ala Lakum Mina Ash-Shajari Al-'Akhḍari Nārāan Fa'idhā 'Antum Minhu Tūqidūna

٨٠ ـ الَّذِي جَعَلَ لَكُمْ مِنَ الشَّجَرِ الْأَخْضَرِ نَارًا فَإِذَا أَنْتُمْ مِنْهُ تُوقِدُونَ

(81) 'Awalaysa Al-Ladhī Khalaqa As-Samāwāti Wa Al-'Arḍa Biqādirin `Alá 'An Yakhluqa Mithlahum Balá Wa Huwa Al-Khallāqu Al-`Alīmu

٨١ ـ أَوَلَيْسَ الَّذِي خَلَقَ السَّمَاوَاتِ وَالْأَرْضَ بِقَادِرٍ عَلَىٰ أَنْ يَخْلُقَ مِثْلَهُمْ ۚ بَلَىٰ وَهُوَ الْخَلَّاقُ الْعَلِيمُ

(82) 'Innamā 'Amruhu 'Idhā 'Arāda Shay'āan 'An Yaqūla Lahu Kun Fayakūnu

٨٢ ـ إِنَّمَا أَمْرُهُ إِذَا أَرَادَ شَيْئًا أَنْ يَقُولَ لَهُ كُنْ فَيَكُونُ

(83) Fasubĥāna Al-Ladhī Biyadihi Malakūtu Kulli Shay'in Wa 'Ilayhi Turja`ūna

٨٣ ـ فَسُبْحَانَ الَّذِي بِيَدِهِ مَلَكُوتُ كُلِّ شَيْءٍ وَإِلَيْهِ تُرْجَعُونَ

Surah Yaseen: Arabic & English meaning

	بِسْمِ اللَّهِ الرَّحْمَٰنِ الرَّحِيمِ
Bismi Allāhi Ar-Raḥmāni Ar-Raḥīmi	

1 Ya, Seen.	١ ـ يس
2 By the Wise Quran.	٢ ـ وَالْقُرْآنِ الْحَكِيمِ
3 You are one of the messengers.	٣ ـ إِنَّكَ لَمِنَ الْمُرْسَلِينَ
4 On a straight path.	٤ ـ عَلَىٰ صِرَاطٍ مُسْتَقِيمٍ
5 The revelation of the Almighty, the Merciful.	٥ ـ تَنْزِيلَ الْعَزِيزِ الرَّحِيمِ
6 To warn a people whose ancestors were not warned, and so they are unaware.	٦ ـ لِتُنْذِرَ قَوْمًا مَا أُنْذِرَ آبَاؤُهُمْ فَهُمْ غَافِلُونَ
7 The Word was realized against most of them, for they do not believe.	٧ ـ لَقَدْ حَقَّ الْقَوْلُ عَلَىٰ أَكْثَرِهِمْ فَهُمْ لَا يُؤْمِنُونَ
8 We placed shackles around their necks, up to their chins, so they are stiff-necked.	٨ ـ إِنَّا جَعَلْنَا فِي أَعْنَاقِهِمْ أَغْلَالًا فَهِيَ إِلَى الْأَذْقَانِ فَهُمْ مُقْمَحُونَ
9 And We placed a barrier in front of them, and a barrier behind them, and We have enshrouded them, so they	٩ ـ وَجَعَلْنَا مِنْ بَيْنِ أَيْدِيهِمْ سَدًّا وَمِنْ خَلْفِهِمْ سَدًّا فَأَغْشَيْنَاهُمْ فَهُمْ لَا يُبْصِرُونَ

cannot see.

10 It is the same for them, whether you warn them, or do not warn them—they will not believe.

١٠ـ وَسَوَاءٌ عَلَيْهِمْ أَأَنْذَرْتَهُمْ أَمْ لَمْ تُنْذِرْهُمْ لَا يُؤْمِنُونَ

11 You warn only him who follows the Message, and fears the Most Gracious inwardly. So give him good news of forgiveness, and a generous reward.

١١ـ إِنَّمَا تُنْذِرُ مَنِ اتَّبَعَ الذِّكْرَ وَخَشِيَ الرَّحْمَٰنَ بِالْغَيْبِ ۖ فَبَشِّرْهُ بِمَغْفِرَةٍ وَأَجْرٍ كَرِيمٍ

12 It is We who revive the dead; and We write down what they have forwarded, and their traces. We have tallied all things in a Clear Record.

١٢ـ إِنَّا نَحْنُ نُحْيِي الْمَوْتَىٰ وَنَكْتُبُ مَا قَدَّمُوا وَآثَارَهُمْ ۚ وَكُلَّ شَيْءٍ أَحْصَيْنَاهُ فِي إِمَامٍ مُبِينٍ

13 And cite for them the parable of the landlords of the town—when the messengers came to it.

١٣ـ وَاضْرِبْ لَهُمْ مَثَلًا أَصْحَابَ الْقَرْيَةِ إِذْ جَاءَهَا الْمُرْسَلُونَ

14 We sent them two messengers, but they denied them both, so We reinforced them with a third. They said, "We are messengers to you."

١٤ـ إِذْ أَرْسَلْنَا إِلَيْهِمُ اثْنَيْنِ فَكَذَّبُوهُمَا فَعَزَّزْنَا بِثَالِثٍ فَقَالُوا إِنَّا إِلَيْكُمْ مُرْسَلُونَ

15 They said, "You are nothing but humans like us, and the Gracious did not send down anything; you are only lying."

١٥ـ قَالُوا مَا أَنْتُمْ إِلَّا بَشَرٌ مِثْلُنَا وَمَا أَنْزَلَ الرَّحْمَٰنُ مِنْ شَيْءٍ إِنْ أَنْتُمْ إِلَّا تَكْذِبُونَ

16 They said, "Our Lord knows that we are messengers to you.

١٦ـ قَالُوا رَبُّنَا يَعْلَمُ إِنَّا إِلَيْكُمْ لَمُرْسَلُونَ

17 And our only duty is clear communication."

١٧ـ وَمَا عَلَيْنَا إِلَّا الْبَلَاغُ الْمُبِينُ

18 They said, "We see an evil omen in you; if you do not give up, we will stone you, and a painful punishment from us will befall you."

١٨ـ قَالُوا إِنَّا تَطَيَّرْنَا بِكُمْ لَئِنْ لَمْ تَنْتَهُوا لَنَرْجُمَنَّكُمْ وَلَيَمَسَّنَّكُمْ مِنَّا عَذَابٌ أَلِيمٌ

19 They said, "Your evil omen is upon you. Is it because you were reminded? But you are an extravagant people."

١٩ـ قَالُوا طَائِرُكُمْ مَعَكُمْ أَئِنْ ذُكِّرْتُمْ بَلْ أَنْتُمْ قَوْمٌ مُسْرِفُونَ

20 Then a man came running from the remotest part of the city. He said, "O my people, follow the messengers.

٢٠ـ وَجَاءَ مِنْ أَقْصَى الْمَدِينَةِ رَجُلٌ يَسْعَىٰ قَالَ يَا قَوْمِ اتَّبِعُوا الْمُرْسَلِينَ

21 Follow those who ask you of no wage, and are themselves guided.

٢١ـ اتَّبِعُوا مَنْ لَا يَسْأَلُكُمْ أَجْرًا وَهُمْ مُهْتَدُونَ

22 "And why should I not worship Him Who created me, and to Whom you will be returned?	٢٢ـ وَمَا لِيَ لَا أَعْبُدُ الَّذِي فَطَرَنِي وَإِلَيْهِ تُرْجَعُونَ
23 Shall I take other gods instead of Him? If the Merciful desires harm for me, their intercession will not avail me at all, nor will they save me.	٢٣ـ أَأَتَّخِذُ مِنْ دُونِهِ آلِهَةً إِنْ يُرِدْنِ الرَّحْمَٰنُ بِضُرٍّ لَا تُغْنِ عَنِّي شَفَاعَتُهُمْ شَيْئًا وَلَا يُنْقِذُونِ
24 In that case, I would be completely lost.	٢٤ـ إِنِّي إِذًا لَفِي ضَلَالٍ مُبِينٍ
25 I have believed in your Lord, so listen to me."	٢٥ـ إِنِّي آمَنْتُ بِرَبِّكُمْ فَاسْمَعُونِ
26 It was said, "Enter Paradise." He said, "If only my people knew.	٢٦ـ قِيلَ ادْخُلِ الْجَنَّةَ قَالَ يَا لَيْتَ قَوْمِي يَعْلَمُونَ
27 How my Lord has forgiven me, and made me one of the honored."	٢٧ـ بِمَا غَفَرَ لِي رَبِّي وَجَعَلَنِي مِنَ الْمُكْرَمِينَ
28 After him, We sent down no hosts from heaven to his people; nor would We ever send any down.	٢٨ـ وَمَا أَنْزَلْنَا عَلَىٰ قَوْمِهِ مِنْ بَعْدِهِ مِنْ جُنْدٍ مِنَ السَّمَاءِ وَمَا كُنَّا مُنْزِلِينَ

29 It was just one Cry, and they were stilled.	٢٩- إِنْ كَانَتْ إِلَّا صَيْحَةً وَاحِدَةً فَإِذَا هُمْ خَامِدُونَ
30 Alas for the servants. No messenger ever came to them, but they ridiculed him.	٣٠- يَا حَسْرَةً عَلَى الْعِبَادِ ۚ مَا يَأْتِيهِمْ مِنْ رَسُولٍ إِلَّا كَانُوا بِهِ يَسْتَهْزِئُونَ
31 Have they not considered how many generations We destroyed before them; and that unto them they will not return?	٣١- أَلَمْ يَرَوْا كَمْ أَهْلَكْنَا قَبْلَهُمْ مِنَ الْقُرُونِ أَنَّهُمْ إِلَيْهِمْ لَا يَرْجِعُونَ
32 All of them, every single one of them, will be arraigned before Us.	٣٢- وَإِنْ كُلٌّ لَمَّا جَمِيعٌ لَدَيْنَا مُحْضَرُونَ
33 And there is a sign for them in the dead land: We give it life, and produce from it grains from which they eat.	٣٣- وَآيَةٌ لَهُمُ الْأَرْضُ الْمَيْتَةُ أَحْيَيْنَاهَا وَأَخْرَجْنَا مِنْهَا حَبًّا فَمِنْهُ يَأْكُلُونَ
34 And We place in it gardens of palm-trees and vines, and cause springs to gush out of it.	٣٤- وَجَعَلْنَا فِيهَا جَنَّاتٍ مِنْ نَخِيلٍ وَأَعْنَابٍ وَفَجَّرْنَا فِيهَا مِنَ الْعُيُونِ
35 That they may eat from its fruits, although their hands did not make it. Will they not be appreciative?	٣٥- لِيَأْكُلُوا مِنْ ثَمَرِهِ وَمَا عَمِلَتْهُ أَيْدِيهِمْ ۖ أَفَلَا يَشْكُرُونَ

36 Glory be to Him who created all the pairs; of what the earth produces, and of their own selves, and of what they do not know.	٣٦ـ سُبْحَانَ الَّذِي خَلَقَ الْأَزْوَاجَ كُلَّهَا مِمَّا تُنْبِتُ الْأَرْضُ وَمِنْ أَنْفُسِهِمْ وَمِمَّا لَا يَعْلَمُونَ
37 Another sign for them is the night: We strip the day out of it—and they are in darkness.	٣٧ـ وَآيَةٌ لَهُمُ اللَّيْلُ نَسْلَخُ مِنْهُ النَّهَارَ فَإِذَا هُمْ مُظْلِمُونَ
38 And the sun runs towards its destination. Such is the design of the Almighty, the All-Knowing.	٣٨ـ وَالشَّمْسُ تَجْرِي لِمُسْتَقَرٍّ لَهَا ۚ ذَٰلِكَ تَقْدِيرُ الْعَزِيزِ الْعَلِيمِ
39 And the moon: We have disposed it in phases, until it returns like the old twig.	٣٩ـ وَالْقَمَرَ قَدَّرْنَاهُ مَنَازِلَ حَتَّىٰ عَادَ كَالْعُرْجُونِ الْقَدِيمِ
40 The sun is not to overtake the moon, nor is the night to outpace the day. Each floats in an orbit.	٤٠ـ لَا الشَّمْسُ يَنْبَغِي لَهَا أَنْ تُدْرِكَ الْقَمَرَ وَلَا اللَّيْلُ سَابِقُ النَّهَارِ ۚ وَكُلٌّ فِي فَلَكٍ يَسْبَحُونَ
41 Another sign for them is that We carried their offspring in the laden Ark.	٤١ـ وَآيَةٌ لَهُمْ أَنَّا حَمَلْنَا ذُرِّيَّتَهُمْ فِي الْفُلْكِ الْمَشْحُونِ
42 And We created for them the like of it, in which they ride.	٤٢ـ وَخَلَقْنَا لَهُمْ مِنْ مِثْلِهِ مَا يَرْكَبُونَ

43 If We will, We can drown them—with no screaming to be heard from them, nor will they be saved.	٤٣ـ وَإِنْ نَشَأْ نُغْرِقْهُمْ فَلَا صَرِيخَ لَهُمْ وَلَا هُمْ يُنْقَذُونَ
44 Except by a mercy from Us, and enjoyment for a while.	٤٤ـ إِلَّا رَحْمَةً مِنَّا وَمَتَاعًا إِلَىٰ حِينٍ
45 Yet when it is said to them, "Beware of what lies before you, and what lies behind you, that you may receive mercy."	٤٥ـ وَإِذَا قِيلَ لَهُمُ اتَّقُوا مَا بَيْنَ أَيْدِيكُمْ وَمَا خَلْفَكُمْ لَعَلَّكُمْ تُرْحَمُونَ
46 Yet never came to them a sign of their Lord's signs, but they turned away from it.	٤٦ـ وَمَا تَأْتِيهِمْ مِنْ آيَةٍ مِنْ آيَاتِ رَبِّهِمْ إِلَّا كَانُوا عَنْهَا مُعْرِضِينَ
47 And when it is said to them, "Spend of what God has provided for you," those who disbelieve say to those who believe, "Shall we feed someone whom God could feed, if He so willed? You must be deeply misguided."	٤٧ـ وَإِذَا قِيلَ لَهُمْ أَنْفِقُوا مِمَّا رَزَقَكُمُ اللَّهُ قَالَ الَّذِينَ كَفَرُوا لِلَّذِينَ آمَنُوا أَنُطْعِمُ مَنْ لَوْ يَشَاءُ اللَّهُ أَطْعَمَهُ إِنْ أَنْتُمْ إِلَّا فِي ضَلَالٍ مُبِينٍ
48 And they say, "When will this promise be, if you are truthful?"	٤٨ـ وَيَقُولُونَ مَتَىٰ هَٰذَا الْوَعْدُ إِنْ كُنْتُمْ صَادِقِينَ
49 All they can expect is a single blast, which will seize them while they feud.	٤٩ـ مَا يَنْظُرُونَ إِلَّا صَيْحَةً وَاحِدَةً تَأْخُذُهُمْ وَهُمْ يَخِصِّمُونَ

50 They will not be able to make a will, nor will they return to their families.	٥٠ـ فَلَا يَسْتَطِيعُونَ تَوْصِيَةً وَلَا إِلَى أَهْلِهِمْ يَرْجِعُونَ
51 The Trumpet will be blown, then behold, they will rush from the tombs to their Lord.	٥١ـ وَنُفِخَ فِي الصُّورِ فَإِذَا هُمْ مِنَ الْأَجْدَاثِ إِلَى رَبِّهِمْ يَنْسِلُونَ
52 They will say, "Woe to us! Who resurrected us from our resting-place?" This is what the Most Gracious had promised, and the messengers have spoken the truth."	٥٢ـ قَالُوا يَا وَيْلَنَا مَنْ بَعَثَنَا مِنْ مَرْقَدِنَا ۜ هَٰذَا مَا وَعَدَ الرَّحْمَٰنُ وَصَدَقَ الْمُرْسَلُونَ
53 It will be but a single scream; and behold, they will all be brought before Us.	٥٣ـ إِنْ كَانَتْ إِلَّا صَيْحَةً وَاحِدَةً فَإِذَا هُمْ جَمِيعٌ لَدَيْنَا مُحْضَرُونَ
54 On that Day, no soul will be wronged in the least, and you will be recompensed only for what you used to do.	٥٤ـ فَالْيَوْمَ لَا تُظْلَمُ نَفْسٌ شَيْئًا وَلَا تُجْزَوْنَ إِلَّا مَا كُنْتُمْ تَعْمَلُونَ
55 The inhabitants of Paradise, on that Day, will be happily busy.	٥٥ـ إِنَّ أَصْحَابَ الْجَنَّةِ الْيَوْمَ فِي شُغُلٍ فَاكِهُونَ
56 They and their spouses, in shades, reclining on couches.	٥٦ـ هُمْ وَأَزْوَاجُهُمْ فِي ظِلَالٍ عَلَى الْأَرَائِكِ مُتَّكِئُونَ

57 They will have therein fruits. They will have whatever they call for.	٥٧ـ لَهُمْ فِيهَا فَاكِهَةٌ وَلَهُمْ مَا يَدَّعُونَ
58 Peace—a saying from a Most Merciful Lord.	٥٨ـ سَلَامٌ قَوْلًا مِنْ رَبٍّ رَحِيمٍ
59 But step aside today, you criminals.	٥٩ـ وَامْتَازُوا الْيَوْمَ أَيُّهَا الْمُجْرِمُونَ
60 Did I not covenant with you, O Children of Adam, that you shall not serve the devil? That he is your sworn enemy?	٦٠ـ أَلَمْ أَعْهَدْ إِلَيْكُمْ يَا بَنِي آدَمَ أَنْ لَا تَعْبُدُوا الشَّيْطَانَ ۖ إِنَّهُ لَكُمْ عَدُوٌّ مُبِينٌ
61 And that you shall serve Me? This is a straight path.	٦١ـ وَأَنِ اعْبُدُونِي ۚ هَٰذَا صِرَاطٌ مُسْتَقِيمٌ
62 He has misled a great multitude of you. Did you not understand?	٦٢ـ وَلَقَدْ أَضَلَّ مِنْكُمْ جِبِلًّا كَثِيرًا ۖ أَفَلَمْ تَكُونُوا تَعْقِلُونَ
63 This is Hellfire, which you were promised.	٦٣ـ هَٰذِهِ جَهَنَّمُ الَّتِي كُنْتُمْ تُوعَدُونَ
64 Roast in it today, because you persistently disbelieved.	٦٤ـ اصْلَوْهَا الْيَوْمَ بِمَا كُنْتُمْ تَكْفُرُونَ

65 On this Day, We will seal their mouths, and their hands will speak to Us, and their feet will testify to everything they had done.	٦٥ـ الْيَوْمَ نَخْتِمُ عَلَىٰ أَفْوَاهِهِمْ وَتُكَلِّمُنَا أَيْدِيهِمْ وَتَشْهَدُ أَرْجُلُهُمْ بِمَا كَانُوا يَكْسِبُونَ
66 If We will, We can blind their eyes as they rush towards the path—but how will they see?	٦٦ـ وَلَوْ نَشَاءُ لَطَمَسْنَا عَلَىٰ أَعْيُنِهِمْ فَاسْتَبَقُوا الصِّرَاطَ فَأَنَّىٰ يُبْصِرُونَ
67 And if We will, We can cripple them in their place; so they can neither move forward, nor go back.	٦٧ـ وَلَوْ نَشَاءُ لَمَسَخْنَاهُمْ عَلَىٰ مَكَانَتِهِمْ فَمَا اسْتَطَاعُوا مُضِيًّا وَلَا يَرْجِعُونَ
68 Whomever We grant old age, We reverse his development. Do they not understand?	٦٨ـ وَمَنْ نُعَمِّرْهُ نُنَكِّسْهُ فِي الْخَلْقِ ۖ أَفَلَا يَعْقِلُونَ
69 We did not teach him poetry, nor is it proper for him. It is only a reminder, and a Clear Quran.	٦٩ـ وَمَا عَلَّمْنَاهُ الشِّعْرَ وَمَا يَنْبَغِي لَهُ ۚ إِنْ هُوَ إِلَّا ذِكْرٌ وَقُرْآنٌ مُبِينٌ
70 That he may warn whoever is alive, and prove the Word against the faithless.	٧٠ـ لِيُنْذِرَ مَنْ كَانَ حَيًّا وَيَحِقَّ الْقَوْلُ عَلَى الْكَافِرِينَ

71 Have they not seen that We created for them, of Our Handiwork, livestock that they own?	٧١ـ أَوَلَمْ يَرَوْا أَنَّا خَلَقْنَا لَهُمْ مِمَّا عَمِلَتْ أَيْدِينَا أَنْعَامًا فَهُمْ لَهَا مَالِكُونَ
72 And We subdued them for them. Some they ride, and some they eat.	٧٢ـ وَذَلَّلْنَاهَا لَهُمْ فَمِنْهَا رَكُوبُهُمْ وَمِنْهَا يَأْكُلُونَ
73 And they have in them other benefits, and drinks. Will they not give thanks?	٧٣ـ وَلَهُمْ فِيهَا مَنَافِعُ وَمَشَارِبُ ۖ أَفَلَا يَشْكُرُونَ
74 Yet they have taken to themselves gods other than God, that perhaps they may be helped.	٧٤ـ وَاتَّخَذُوا مِنْ دُونِ اللَّهِ آلِهَةً لَعَلَّهُمْ يُنْصَرُونَ
75 They cannot help them, although they are arrayed as troops for them.	٧٥ـ لَا يَسْتَطِيعُونَ نَصْرَهُمْ وَهُمْ لَهُمْ جُنْدٌ مُحْضَرُونَ
76 So let their words not sadden you. We know what they conceal, and what they reveal.	٧٦ـ فَلَا يَحْزُنْكَ قَوْلُهُمْ ۘ إِنَّا نَعْلَمُ مَا يُسِرُّونَ وَمَا يُعْلِنُونَ
77 Does the human being not consider that We created him from a seed? Yet he becomes a fierce adversary.	٧٧ـ أَوَلَمْ يَرَ الْإِنْسَانُ أَنَّا خَلَقْنَاهُ مِنْ نُطْفَةٍ فَإِذَا هُوَ خَصِيمٌ مُبِينٌ

78 And he produces arguments against Us, and he forgets his own creation. He says, "Who will revive the bones when they have decayed?"	٧٨ـ وَضَرَبَ لَنَا مَثَلًا وَنَسِيَ خَلْقَهُ ۖ قَالَ مَنْ يُحْيِي الْعِظَامَ وَهِيَ رَمِيمٌ
79 Say, "He who initiated them in the first instance will revive them. He has knowledge of every creation."	٧٩ـ قُلْ يُحْيِيهَا الَّذِي أَنْشَأَهَا أَوَّلَ مَرَّةٍ ۖ وَهُوَ بِكُلِّ خَلْقٍ عَلِيمٌ
80 He who produced fuel for you from the green trees, with which you kindle a fire.	٨٠ـ الَّذِي جَعَلَ لَكُمْ مِنَ الشَّجَرِ الْأَخْضَرِ نَارًا فَإِذَا أَنْتُمْ مِنْهُ تُوقِدُونَ
81 Is not He who created the heavens and the earth able to create the like of them? Certainly. He is the Supreme All-Knowing Creator.	٨١ـ أَوَلَيْسَ الَّذِي خَلَقَ السَّمَاوَاتِ وَالْأَرْضَ بِقَادِرٍ عَلَىٰ أَنْ يَخْلُقَ مِثْلَهُمْ ۚ بَلَىٰ وَهُوَ الْخَلَّاقُ الْعَلِيمُ
82 His command, when He wills a thing, is to say to it, "Be," and it comes to be.	٨٢ـ إِنَّمَا أَمْرُهُ إِذَا أَرَادَ شَيْئًا أَنْ يَقُولَ لَهُ كُنْ فَيَكُونُ
83 So glory be to Him in whose hand is the dominion of everything, and to Him you will be returned.	٨٣ـ فَسُبْحَانَ الَّذِي بِيَدِهِ مَلَكُوتُ كُلِّ شَيْءٍ وَإِلَيْهِ تُرْجَعُونَ

Surah Yaseen: Benefits

Benefits Of Reading Surah Yasin

Surah **Yasin**, also written as **Ya-Sin** and **Yaseen**, is the 36th Surah (chapter) of the Quran and contains 83 verses. For those who don't know what is Yasin Shareef, it is the heart of the Quran as it mentions all six articles or root beliefs of Islam, including belief in only one God, belief in prophethood, and belief in after-life and resurrection, among others.

Surah Yaseen is one of the most loved Surah of the Holy Quran. Its recitation and memorization hold high importance. And it is a source of great reward too. The recitation of Surah Yaseen helps us in attaining Allah's forgiveness too. Indeed, every letter of the Holy Quran is filled with mercy, blessings, and rewards.

It was narrated that Anas (Radi Allahu Anhu) said: "The Messenger of Allah (PBUH) said:

"Everything has a heart and the heart of the Quran is Yaseen. Whoever recites Surah Yaseen, Allah will record for him the reward of reading the Quran ten times."

(Jami At-Tirmidhi, 2887)

Importance Of Surah Yaseen

Surah Yaseen is the 36th Surah of the Quran. It was revealed to Prophet Muhammad in Mecca; hence it is a Meccan (Makki) Surah. It has 83 verses, 730 words, and 3,068 letters. It is divided into 5 sections. Its name is also derived from two letters (Hurrof Al Muqattat) and Allah knows the best about its meaning. SubhanAllah! Indeed, Allah is the Knower of All things. This Surah is filled with hidden treasures that one attains by reciting and memorizing it.

- "Everything has a heart, and the heart of the Quran is Surah Yasin; whoever reads it, it is as if he has read the Quran ten times."
- "Whoever reads Surah Yasin in one night will be forgiven in the morning."
- "Whoever recites Surah Yaseen at night seeking Allah's approval, Allah would forgive him."
- "Whoever continues to read it every night then dies, will die as a shaheed (martyr)."
- "Whoever enters the graveyard and reads Surah Yasin, their (punishment) will be reduced that day, and he will have Hasanaat (reward) equal to the number of people in the graveyard."

The Prophet (PBUH) said:

"Whoever reads Surah Yaseen seeking Allah's pleasure, his past sins will be forgiven. So recite it over the dying among you."
(Jami' Al Sagheer, 5785)

Undoubtedly, there is a blessing in every Surah of the Quran that we do not even know. We can never imagine the blessings and rewards that Surah Yaseen can bring upon us. It is important for us to recite a lot of the Quran as stated in the Hadith:

The prophet (PBUH) also said:

"The one who was devoted to the Quran will be told (on the Day of Resurrection) 'Recite (the Quran) and ascend (in the ranks) as you used to recite when you were in the world. Your rank will be at the last verse you recite."

(Abu Dawood and jami –At-Tirmidhi).

SubhanAllah! Such is the importance. And Surah Yaseen is filled with the glory of Allah, his Hidaayah, and Mercy.

Another Hadith that glorifies the importance of Surah Yaseen is:

"Allah recited Ta-Ha and Yaseen one thousand years before He created the heavens and the earth. When the angels heard the Qur'an they said, 'Glad tidings to the nation to whom this will be revealed, and glad tidings to the hearts that will bear this, and glad tidings to the tongues that will speak these words."

(Sunan Ad-Darimi, 3280)

Messege In Surah Yaseen

Indeed, Allah has sent us many signs and one of the signs is the Quran. Allah SWT mentions the Prophethood of Muhammad (PBUH) in Surah Yaseen. So that he (PBUH) can warn people. This Surah also states about wrongdoers that their necks will be chained on the Day of Judgment. Reciting this Surah makes us realize that whatsoever we do, there is a clear register that maintains our deeds. This Surah very clearly mentions the signs of Allah, the Greatness of Allah, the last day when the trumpet will be blown, and when our body parts will advocate our deeds.

Lessons In Surah Yaseen

Surah Yaseen tells us about the story of three (2+1) prophets that were sent by Allah SWT. But the whole city denied them except one person. He called them towards the truth with courage. However, the people of that city killed him. However, Allah admitted him to paradise for his sacrifice. SubhanAllah.

Moral: This story teaches us that we might be alone on the path of Allah. But we should not lose courage but stand firmly. It's because the reward from Allah will be unimaginably great. It also teaches us that this life is a mere test and it's the afterlife that's our final abode. It also makes us ponder upon the fact that Allah is so Merciful that He sent not one, two, but three prophets for guidance. Yet, the people of that city preferred falsehood over truth. Hence, we should make strong connections with Allah SWT, realize his signs, and always be on the path of faith.

Great Benefits Of Surah Yaseen

1. Reading Surah Yaseen fulfills your every need

The Prophet (PBUH) said:

"Whoever reads Surah Yaseen at the beginning of the day; his needs will be fulfilled." (Mishkat al Masaabih; 2118)

Another hadith states that:
"Whoever reads Surah Yaseen is forgiven; whoever reads it in hunger is satisfied; whoever reads it having lost their way, finds their way; whoever reads it on losing an animal, finds it. When one reads it apprehending that their food will run short, that food becomes sufficient. If one reads it beside a person who is in the throes of death, these are made easy for them. If anyone reads it on a woman experiencing difficulty in childbirth, her delivery becomes easy."

2. Reading Surah Yaseen will get our sins forgiven

A Hadith states that:

The Prophet (PBUH) said: **"Whoever recited Surah Yaseen in the night seeking Allah's pleasure, Allah would forgive him."**
(Sunan Ad-Darimi: 3283/A)

We must also not forget that reading and reciting the Quran in this worldly life will intercede for us on Judgment day. Hence, reciting Surah Yaseen a lot will make us worthy of that reward anyway.

3. Reciting Surah Yaseen will help you attain martyrdom

The Prophet (PBUH) said:

"Whoever continues to read Surah Yaseen every night then dies, will die as a shaheed (martyr)." (Tabarani)

4. Reading Surah Yaseen helps us attain great rewards in the holy month of Ramadan

The Prophet (PBUH) said:

"Whosoever reads the heart of the Quran- "Yaseen" in Ramadan will receive the Sawaab of reading 10 Qurans."
(Jami –At-Tirmidhi)

We should recite lots and lots of Surah Yaseen in the month of Ramadan to make the most out of the holy month.

5. Reciting Surah Yaseen saves the deceased from the torment and helps gain hasanat

Narrated by Al-Tha'labi (R.A) in his Tafseer:

Narrated from Anas Ibn Malik (Radi Allahu Anhu) who said that the Messenger of Allah (Sallallahu Alayhi Wasallam) said:
"Whoever enters the graveyard and recites Surah Yaa-Seen, (the torment) will be reduced for them that day, and he will have Hasanat equivalent to the number of people in the graveyard."

Another Hadith in Musnad of Ahmad, Sunan Abu Dawood, Sunan Nasa'i & Mustadrak Al Hakim states that:

Ma'qil Ibn Yasar (Radi Allahu Anhu) relates that the Messenger of Allah (Sallallahu Alayhi Wasallam) said,

"Surah Yasin is the heart of the Qur'an. No one reads it intending thereby Allah and the Next Abode except that Allah forgives them. Recite it for your deceased ones."

6. Surah Yaseen is filled with guidance and lessons

Deep reflection over Surah Yaseen trembles the heart of a believer. It is a Surah that guides us to see the signs of Allah SWT. It also makes us aware of the last day and that everything we do is recorded. And also, our every action will come in front of us on Judgment day. Nevertheless, it is a part of the Quran which is the greatest source of guidance.

"This Quran is a clear statement to [all] the people and a guidance and instruction for those conscious of Allah."

(Surah Aal-i-Imraan: 138)

7. Its lesson will keep us on the path of righteousness

Reciting and memorizing Surah Yaseen will keep our faith fresh and help us be on the path of righteousness even when the world burdens us with hardships and obsta

8. Reciting Surah Yaseen in the morning will be beneficial

It will be a good start to the day if we recite a part of the Quran in the morning. Reciting Surah Yaseen in the morning and pondering upon its meaning will keep us aware of Allah and its signs throughout the day.

"Establish prayer at the decline of the sun [from its median] until the darkness of the night and [also] the Quran of dawn. Indeed, the recitation of dawn is ever witnessed."

(Surah Al-Israel:78)

9. Reciting Surah Yaseen will help us stay away from sins

The deep message of Last Day and the continuous reminder of our records being maintained can help us stay away from the sins. Reading and Reciting Surah Yaseen every day will act as a daily reminder. It will also soften our hearts and make us closer to Allah.

10. The benefit of reciting Surah Yaseen on a Friday Evening

A hadith in Sunan Baihaqi states that:

"Whoever reads Surah Yaseen on the eve of Friday will be forgiven in the morning."

Reading Surah Yaseen After Fajr

Reading Surah Yaseen has several benefits that could be bestowed upon the reader once he/she reads the Surah. Despite there are many benefits of reciting Surah Yaseen in the morning, the hadith mentioned in hadiths are two:

– Allah (SWT) accepts one's Dua and fulfills his/ her needs.

This was mentioned above in the previous point. Prophet Muhammad (PBUH) said,

"One who recites Surah Yaseen in the morning, Allah Almighty will be responsible for fulfilling all his needs."

– Allah (SWT) forgives our sins, Prophet Muhammad (PBUH) said:

"One who recites Surah Yaseen in the morning or night, Allah Almighty would remove all his sins." [7]

Reading Surah Yaseen For Marriage

From what has been previously mentioned, it is recommended for every Muslim who is going to have a marriage to read Surah Yaseen, with the intention that Allah (SWT) guides us to the right choice, and make our marriage blessed and has no complications.

Reading Surah Yaseen During Pregnancy

Pregnancy is a very tough period for all mothers. During these hard weeks, mothers should seek Allah's help and support for their fetus and her, as well. Reading Surah Yaseen and making Dua after reciting it will definitely ease this time for both of them.

Tips To Memorize Surah Yaseen

Memorization of Surah Yaseen is one of the noblest thoughts. Indeed, it is a special surah of the Quran.

- Make strong niyyah to memorize Surah Yaseen.
- Set a dedicated time to work on its memorization, pronunciation, and phonetics.
- Memorize it after Fajr prayer and make time to revise the learned segments on a Friday Eve.
- Take help from a Quran teacher online to work on your Tajweed and get better efficiency.

Dua After Reading Surah Yasin

There is no accurate Hadith about dua after Yasin, but it is believed that any dua offered after reciting Surah Yasin will be accepted by the mercy of Allah Almighty. Let us see some short and meaningful dua that can be recited after Surah Yasin:

Dua: Alhamdu lillahii 'ala kulli ne'matin wa astaghfirullaha min kulli zambin,wa asaluhu min kulli khairin,wa a'udhu billahi min kulli sharrin
Translation: Praise be to Allah for all the blessings. Oh Allah, Forgive all our sins, give us all that is good and keep us away from all that is bad.

Dua: Allahumma inni asaluka wal amna wal eemaana fid-dunya wal aakher
Translation: O Allah I ask of You peace & faith in this world and in the hereafter.

Dua: Allaahu, Allaahu, Rabbi Ar-Rahmanur-Raheemu, Laa ushriku bihi shay'aa
Translation: Allah, Allah, my Lord, the Most Gracious [and] the Most Merciful I do not associate anything with Him.

Dua: Yaa may-yakfee min kulli shayin walaa yakfee minhu shayun ikfinee maa ahammanee mimaa anaa feehi
Translation: O He who is sufficient from all things but nothing is sufficient from Him. Be sufficient for me in what worries me in the state I am.

For more books and exercise books, activities or coloring books in Arabic or Islamic, please visit our author page: "**Aicha Mhamed**"
You have also found a book that talks about Islam history, Ramadan and others.

Made in the USA
Las Vegas, NV
19 July 2023

74974815R00024